THE TWO KINGS
a chess story

by
PAUL SCHARFF

in cooperation with
GUSTAVO MINACCI

CADOGAN
chess

Once upon a time, a very long time ago, there was a king. His name was King Kashem, and he ruled over a small country far away in India. One day he sat in his palace looking gloomily out of the window. In the hills he could see his army gathering together its forces. Elephants and soldiers with all their weapons were about to set out for the border to defend the kingdom.

Kashem was certainly not the kind of king who likes going
to war, which explained why he was so gloomy.
But it looked as though he had no choice.
The cruel King Baduraul's army was about to attack
the fertile valley of the river Chenab.

That morning Baduraul came in person to the palace of King Kashem in order to declare war on him. With a clomping of boots and a rattling of weapons he and his men stormed into the king's throne room.

'That valley belongs to me!' was the first thing Baduraul shouted.

'It is a game, your Majesty. You are both sure to like it. It is a sort of peaceful war, called chess. You need two armies of chess pieces, and a board on which to fight the battle. You could command one of the armies, Sire, and King Baduraul the other.'

Kashem tried as calmly as he could to persuade him otherwise, but after each argument he presented, Baduraul only replied: 'That valley belongs to me!'

It was obvious that King Baduraul was not interested in talking – he wanted to fight! King Kashem's last hopes of avoiding war were dashed. Now everybody was shouting at once in front of his throne.

In the commotion nobody noticed that a small boy had squeezed his way to the front, and now stood near the two kings. He tugged at the king's sleeve and cried: 'Sire, I know a way to avoid this war!'

'And just what did you have in mind, Kalem?' asked King Kashem, recognising him to be the son of the court steward.

The two kings looked at one another uncertainly.

Kalem went on: 'It is a war in which the one who thinks of the best ideas, manoeuvers his army the best, and is the cleverest, wins.'

'That sounds very good,' said Kashem. 'What do you think, Baduraul?'

'This game also interests me,' growled Baduraul, who was quite sure that nobody was cleverer than he was. 'But I will only play if the prize for the winner is the valley of the Chenab!'

'Teach us how to play this chess game, Kalem, and we will play for the valley of the Chenab,' promised King Kashem.

Both kings were sure that they would win, and they both wanted to make sure the other could not back out if he lost.

'If I win, that valley is mine, Kashem!' cried the first.

'Yes, but if I win, you must withdraw your army, and you may never declare war again!' replied the other.

'Take your places at the table, your Majesties, and we can begin the lessons,' called Kalem.

He put the chess board on the table. 'This is the battlefield,' he said.

The two kings looked at one another fiercely.

'On your own side of the board you should always have a white square on your right,' continued Kalem.

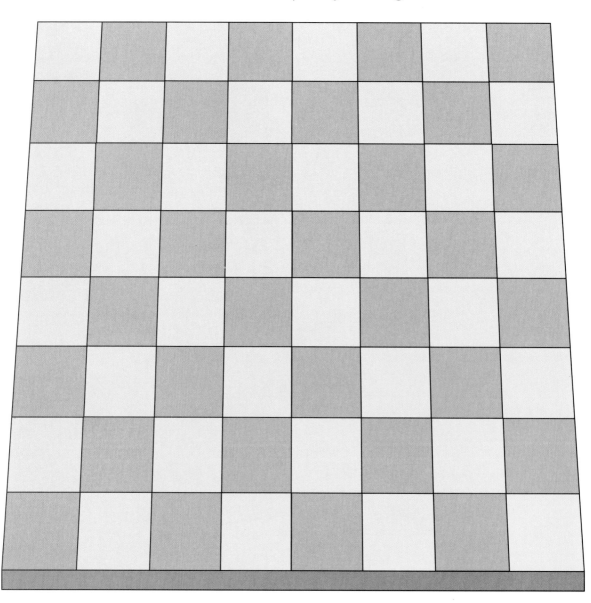

'There are 32 white (light) squares and 32 black (dark) squares altogether. The pieces can move across the board in several different ways.' There are three important paths.

Files: Some pieces move vertically along so-called *files*. Files run up and down the board between the opposing sides.

Ranks: Other pieces move horizontally along so-called *ranks*, which run from side to side across the width of the board.

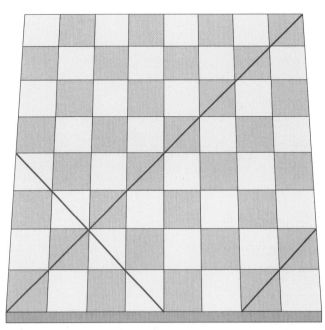

Diagonals: There are also pieces that move along the so-called *diagonals*. Diagonals are slanting rows which cross the board at an angle.

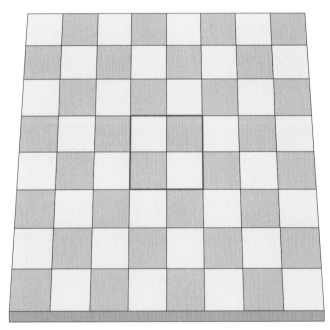

The four midboard squares are called the **center.** You should always bear this in mind as the pieces located here have the chance to move along very important paths!

'Kalem,' said King Kashem impatiently, 'I want to know what my army looks like.' 'Of course, Sire. I will show you,' answered Kalem.

the armies

Each army will have:

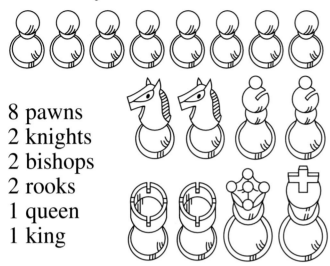

8 pawns
2 knights
2 bishops
2 rooks
1 queen
1 king

'Can we get started?' asked King Baduraul, impatient as ever.
'I still haven't explained the rules of the game,' said Kalem a bit nervously. 'Let us begin by setting up the board.'

The pieces are placed on the first and the last two ranks. We put the rooks in the corners, next to them the knights, then the bishops, and the king and the queen on the remaining two squares. Make sure that the queen stands on a square of her own colour; in other words the white queen on a white square and the black queen on a black square.
We place the pawns on the second and the seventh ranks, in front of the pieces. Make sure that the board is always placed so that the lower left corner is a black square, and the lower right corner a white square.
'I shall now explain how each of the pieces can move,' continued Kalem.

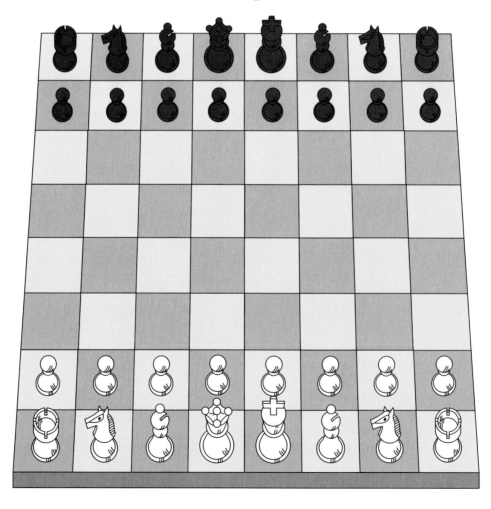

the rook

Let us begin with the rook.

At the start of the game the rooks are positioned at the four corners of the board. They are rather like look-out towers. Just as a tower provides you with a view of the surrounding fields, the village or the town, the rooks look out over all the squares of the chess board.

You can move the rook as many squares as you like in one move, but only along ranks (horizontal) or files (vertical).

In the *diagram* alongside, the red dots show all the squares the rook can reach in a single move.

The rook is one of the most precious possessions of its king and can be a powerful weapon.

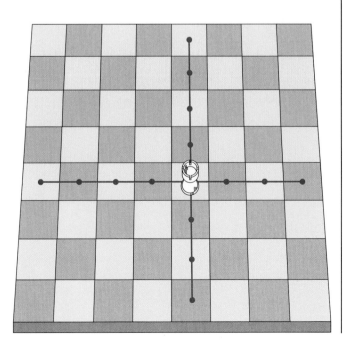

the bishop

Now we come to the bishop.

At the beginning of the game the four bishops stand next to the king and the queen. The bishop is the king's adviser and messenger. He takes the king's wishes and commands to the most distant parts of the chess board.

'Then he must be able to move very fast,' said Baduraul.

'Yes, he is one of the fastest of all pieces. He moves along the diagonals (slanting rows) of the board, as many squares as you like in one move.'

In the *diagram* alongside, the red dots show all the squares that the bishop can reach in a single move from a random position at the centre of the board.

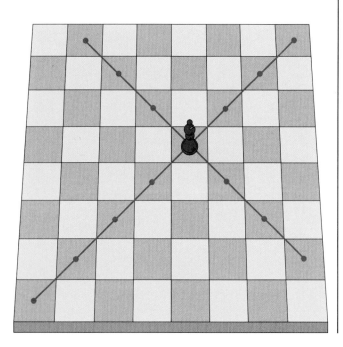

the queen

The next piece is the queen.

At the start of the game the queen stands proudly alongside her king. She is the piece with the most power. She leads both the attack and the defence, and is involved in almost every single skirmish. That means she has to be able to move over the board in every possible way: vertically up and down the files, horizontally across the ranks, and diagonally along the slanting rows.

'Aha, in other words just like a rook and a bishop combined into one,' said Baduraul.

'Correct,' replied Kalem.

In the *diagram* alongside, the red dots indicate which squares the queen can reach in a single move.

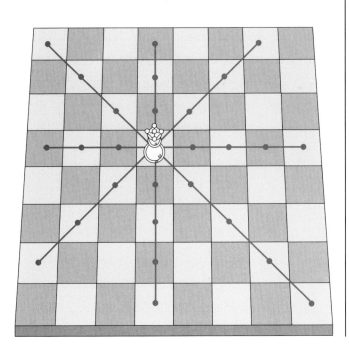

the king

'And now for the king!' cried Kashem and Baduraul in chorus. 'Those other pieces are all very interesting, but we ourselves are kings, and it is about time you told us how we move.' 'I was going to save the most important piece for last, Sires,' said Kalem, 'but since you insist ...'

The king is the piece that everything else revolves around. At the start of the game he stands next to the queen in the middle of the first rank, surrounded by his army. If he is captured, the game is over, and your opponent has won.

That is why the king has to move cautiously. Naturally enough, he can move in all directions, just like the queen, but only one step at a time; in other words just one square per move. The red dots in the *diagram* show which squares the king can reach in a single move.

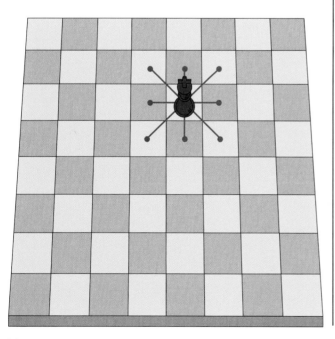

14

the knight

Now it is the knight's turn.

At the start of the game each knight stands between a rook and a bishop, mounted and ready for action.

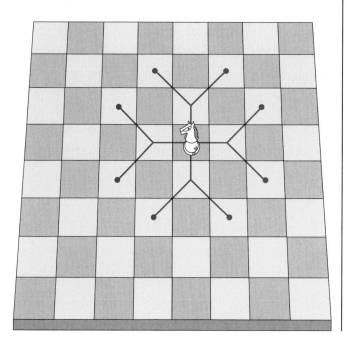

The use of knights on horseback makes an army much more mobile. The knight is the only piece that can jump over other pieces. Beginners at chess sometimes find the way the knight moves a bit difficult; the easiest way to describe it is 'one straight, one diagonal,' in other words move one square horizontally or vertically, then one more diagonally.

Look carefully at the *diagram* again to help you understand how the knight moves; the red dots tell you which squares the knight can reach in a single move.

He always changes square colour when he moves, going from white to black or from black to white.

the pawn

Now, last but not least, the pawns. There are common soldiers on the chessboard just as there are in every army. At the start of the game they are placed protectively on the second rank in front of the other pieces.

The pawns definitely do not have it easy; there are eight of them, but they are always at the spearhead of the attack. Another big headache for the pawns is that they can only move forward, and they are never allowed to turn back.

On his very first move, each pawn has the choice of going either one or two squares forward, but after that he can only move one square at a time.

In the *diagram* the red dots show you exactly which squares the pawns can reach in a single move.

In diagrams white pawns can only go up and the black pawns down.

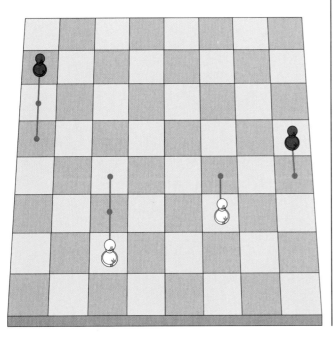

exercises

Dot all the squares that can be reached in a single move by all the pieces present in the chessboard. Look at the example in the first diagram.

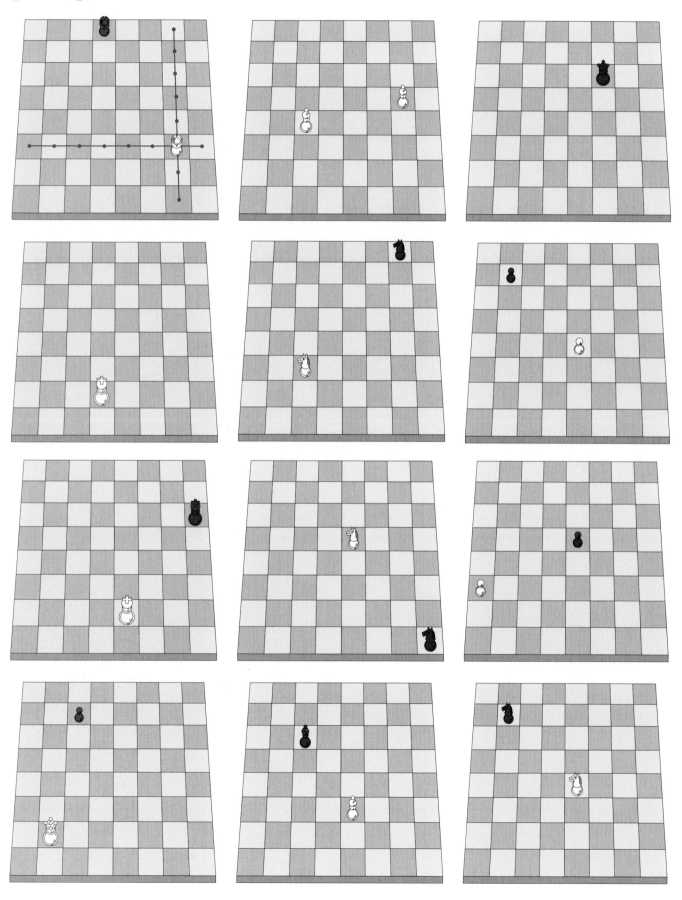

capturing pieces

'Kalem, if all the pieces and pawns charge forward, then they will meet somewhere in the middle and get completely stuck. What do we do then?' asked King Kashem.

'If you want to move a piece and find that one of your opponent's pieces is in the way, then you can capture his piece and place yours on the square where his piece was standing. White pieces can capture black pieces, and black can capture white.' 'Can pawns capture pieces as well?' 'Certainly, all the pieces can capture opponent's pieces when they are in range.'

In the *diagram* below, you see how a rook captures a knight.

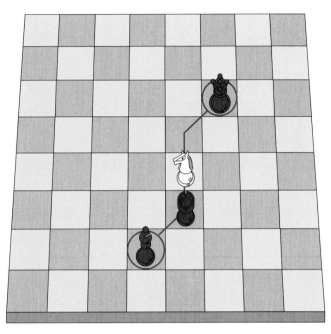

In the following *diagram,* you see a bishop capturing a pawn.

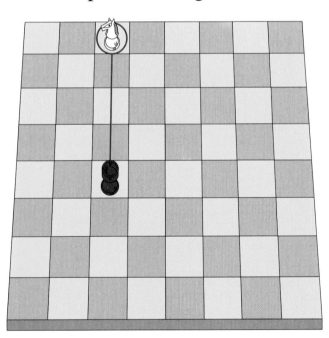

The knight is the only piece that can jump over other pieces. The white knight can capture the queen or the bishop, even though it has to jump over the black rook (next *diagram*).

The pawn is the only piece that does not move in its usual way when capturing a piece. To take a piece, the pawn moves diagonally forward instead of straight ahead, and never more than one square at a time even if it is his first move! In the following *diagram* you see a white pawn taking a rook.

18

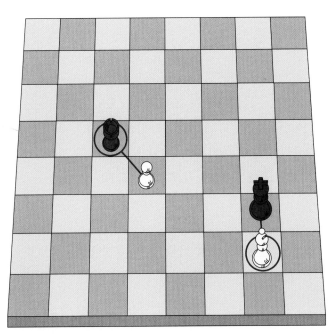 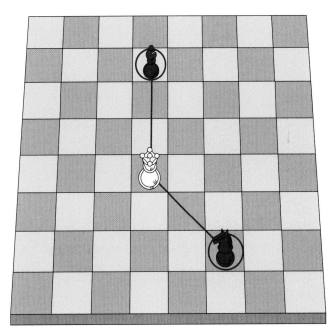

In the *diagram* to the left you see the pawn capturing the rook and the king taking the bishop. The king can also capture! In the *diagram* to the right, you see how the queen can either take a bishop on the same line, or move diagonally to take a knight. Of course you can only take one piece per move, so you have to make a choice!

exercises

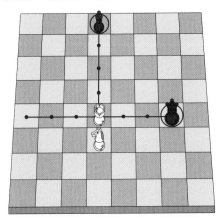

The example shows all the moves and captures the rook can make.

Mark all the moves and captures the black bishop can make.

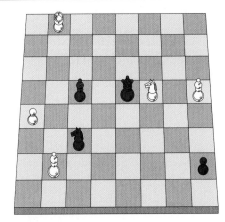

Mark all the moves and captures the black queen can make.

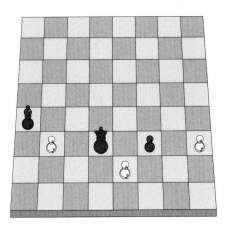

Mark all the moves and captures the white pawns can make.

Mark all the moves and captures the white knight can make.

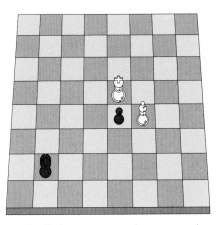

Mark all the moves and captures the white king can make.

what can the pieces do?

As the soldiers of your army, the chess pieces will need to work hard and be very brave to win the battle. We have learnt that some of them are more powerful than others, depending on the way they move. However, pieces can perform five very important tasks during the game. King Kashem asked: 'Is a simple pawn also capable to perform these five tasks?'

'Sure,' said Kalem, 'the pawn can move, capture, threaten, defend and control.'

Let's look carefully at each one of them.

moving

All the pieces have their own way of moving over the board. You can see the knight's moves in the *diagram* besides.

Remember, the knight is the only one that can jump over the pieces.

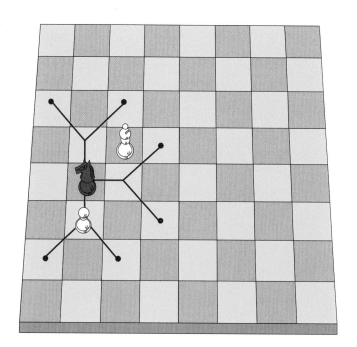

capturing

It is very important to take the opponent's pieces, so that you take away the opponent's king protection. In the example, the knight can capture the queen and the pawn can take the rook. Remember, the pawn is the only piece that moves differently when capturing.

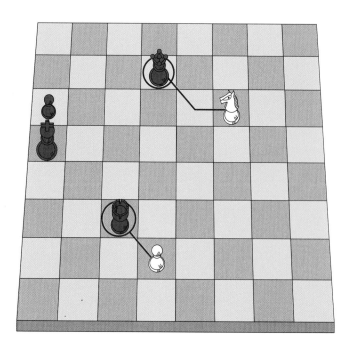

threatening

A piece is threatened if it is standing on a square where it can be captured. In the *diagram,* the white queen is threatening the black pawn.

'This is what I have to do to capture Kashem's pieces!' thought King Baduraul.

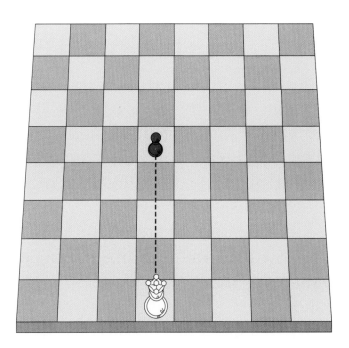

defending

Pieces of the same colour can defend one another. When your opponent takes one of your pieces which is defended, you can then take his piece back!

In the board to the right, the knight is defending the pawn, ready to punish the queen if she captures it.

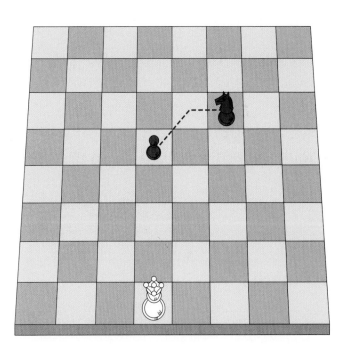

controlling

Pieces can dominate or control some of the squares and paths of the board. Look carefully at the example: the rook controls one file and one rank, 14 squares in total. All these squares can be reached in one move. If an opponent's piece steps onto one of these squares, you can capture it.

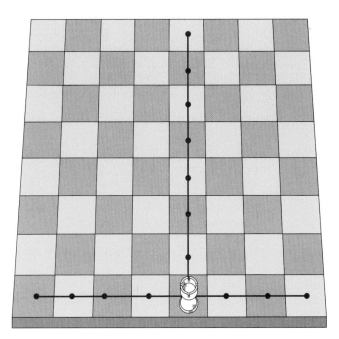

check and checkmate

'Kalem, how do you actually win the game?' asked King Baduraul.

'The only way you can win is by capturing the opponent's king,' answered Kalem.

If you threaten the opponent's king, that is called putting him in check, and you must say 'Check!' out loud.

King Kashem interrupted Kalem, and asked while putting the pieces in place as they are in the diagram: 'If I move the bishop and put the black king in check, does that mean I win?'

'No, just putting your opponent in check is not enough to win,' said

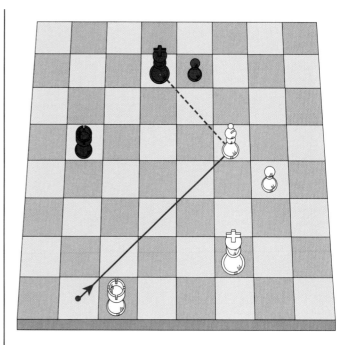

Kalem. 'The black king can still get out of check.'

Let's see how.

---

how to get out of check

1. The checking piece may be captured.

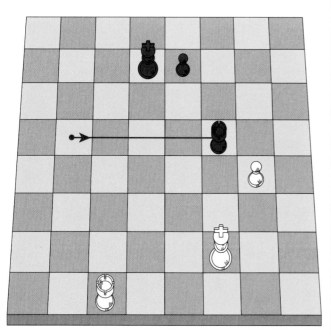

The rook saves his king by taking the bishop.

2. A piece may be placed between the checking piece and the king.

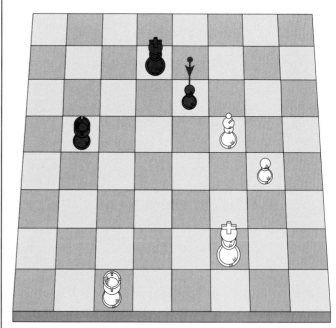

The black pawn protects his king from the enemy bishop.

22

3. The king may move to a square where he is no longer attacked.

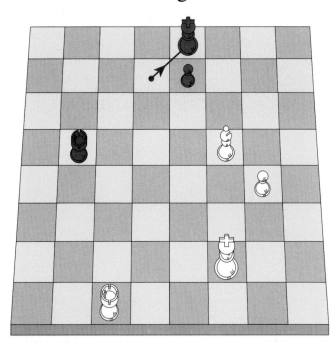

The king moves one square sideways.

When the king is threatened, he and his army have to come up with one of these three solutions.

things that are not allowed

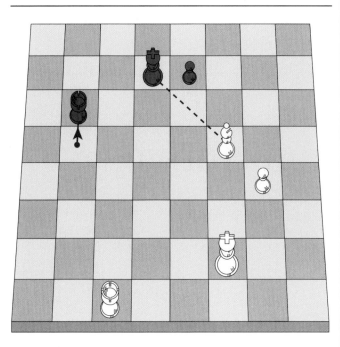

You are not allowed to abandon your king by making a move which will leave him in check.

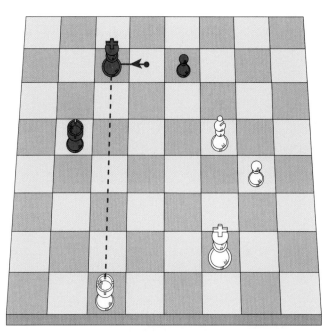

You are not allowed to move the king to a square which is controlled by an opponent's piece; if you did, you would be putting yourself in check!

exercises

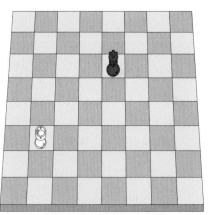

Move the white rook
to put your opponent in check.

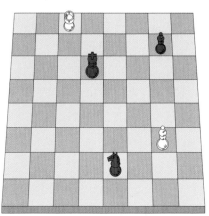

Find all the possible alternatives
to get the black king out of check.

'But, Kalem, you still haven't told us how we can win the game!' cried King Baduraul.

'Let's go back to the previous position, where the bishop is checking the black king,' said Kalem. 'Let's imagine the black king gets out of check moving to the black square above him:

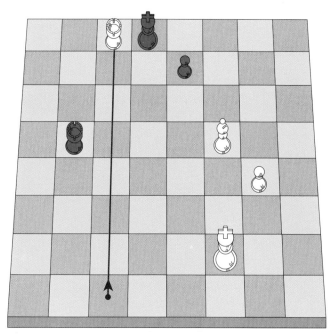

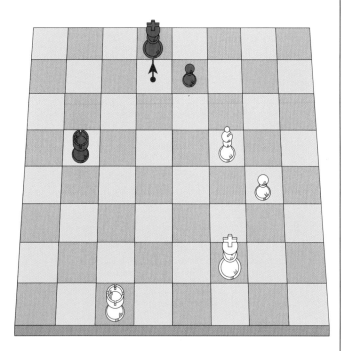

Now we put the black king in check by moving the white rook to the square next to the king.'

What happens now?

The rook which has put the king in

check also sees to it that the black king has no more squares to escape to. The king cannot take the rook, because it is protected by the white bishop. He cannot go anywhere!

This is what we call checkmate; the king is in check, and there is no way he can get out of it. The game is over and white has won.

Remember! The king can never actually be taken, but his fate is what determines who wins the game. The king must be defended to the bitter end.

the three special moves

castling

'If you look at the opening position, don't you think the king is very unsafe there in the middle?' asked King Baduraul. 'I think he would be much safer over in the corner next to the rook.'

'That has been considered, Sire,' answered Kalem.

In order to provide the king with extra protection, you can *castle*. This is a special move which takes the king to a safer place. In this one special move, you are able to move two pieces at once – namely the king and the rook.

Castling takes place as follows:

The king moves two squares towards one of his rooks, then the rook jumps over the king and stops on the square next to him.

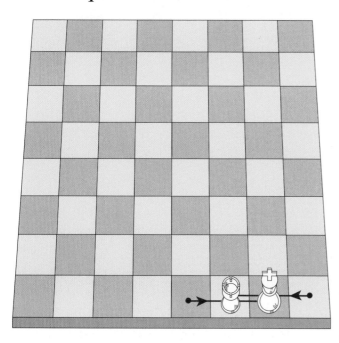

This is how you castle on the king's side. 'Can you castle with either rook?' asked Kashem. 'Sure! Rooks have a duty to protect the king.'

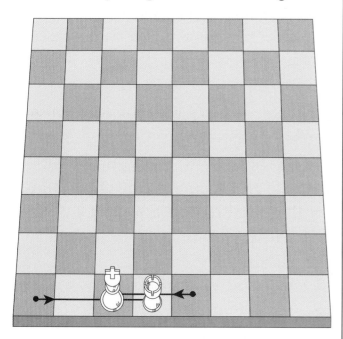

This is how you castle on the queen's side, so that the king ends up a bit more towards the middle of the board. The king always moves two squares first, and then the rook

jumps over him. Castling on the side of the queen is called *castling long,* and on the side of the king *castling short.*

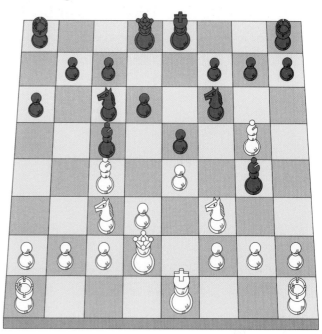

Here white can castle long or short, black can only castle short.

the four castling rules

1. You can only castle with the king and a rook when neither piece has been moved earlier in the game.

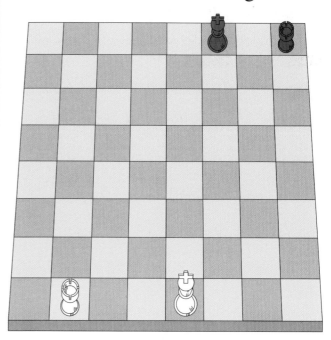

Here neither white nor black can castle any more.

2. The king that wants to castle must not be in check.

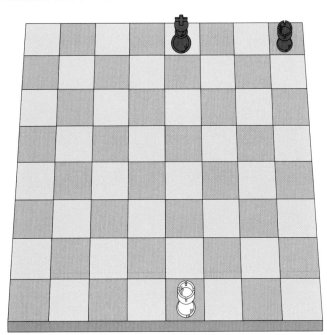

Here black is not allowed to castle to get out of check.

3. You may not castle if the king has to pass over a square that is threatened by one of the opponent's pieces during the castling move.

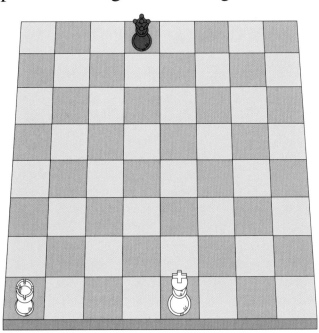

White is not allowed to castle on the queen's side because the black queen is controlling the square which the white king has to cross.

4. The king must not finish up in check after castling.

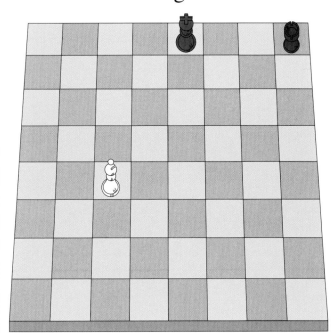

If black castled in this situation, he would end up in check from the white bishop. That means he is not allowed to castle.

---

capturing en passant

It took Kashem and Baduraul quite a while to get used to the idea of castling, which is why Kalem is a bit hesitant when he said: 'There is one other very special move in chess. Only this time it is not made by the most important of the pieces, but rather by the most ordinary – the pawn.'

When a pawn moves two squares on its first move, ending up directly alongside one of the opponent's pawns, then your opponent can treat your pawn just as if it had moved only one square forward. Which means he can capture it! But he must do so straight away, and not wait for the next move because then it is too late.

This special way in which pawns can capture one another is called capturing 'en passant', which is French for 'in passing' – and 'capturing in passing' is exactly what happens in this move.

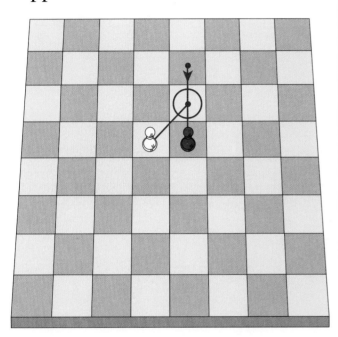

In this *diagram* you see how the black pawn advances two squares on its first move, finishing up alongside a white pawn. The white pawn can now capture the black pawn 'en passant'.

pawn promotion

'This sort of thing makes it very difficult for our pawns to gain a bit of ground,' said King Kashem. 'It is hard for them to move forward, and when they do, they cannot turn back. That makes them very weak, it seems to me.'

'You are quite right, Sire,' answered Kalem. 'It is very difficult for a pawn to get into enemy territory.

But if he does succeed in reaching the other side of the board, there is a big reward waiting for him.'

The pawn that is brave enough to battle all the way to the other side of the board is given a new life, and he can choose for himself what he wants to become!

Of course there is only one king of each colour, so he cannot become the king.

But apart from that, he can become whatever he likes: a queen, a rook, a knight or a bishop. It is very likely that he will want to become a queen, since the queen is the strongest of the pieces.

The white pawn is promoted to become one of these pieces.

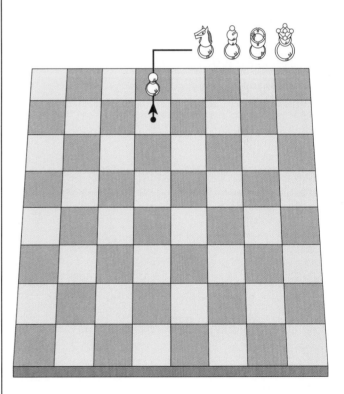

When a pawn reaches the last rank, it has to be taken off the board and replaced by the chosen piece!

A table was placed on a hilltop near the palace,
and there the two kings took their places.
Their two armies looked on rather uneasily.
Was there going to be a battle or not?
Little Kalem put the board on the table,
so that each king had a white square on his right, and
then respectfully stepped back a few paces.

the game

The explanations were over. Now the two opponents knew all the rules of the game.

'I declare war on you, here on the chess board,' growled Baduraul, who had always been good at games. 'I am going to beat you, Kashem, and then the valley of the river Chenab will be mine forever!'

white

You will notice that next to each diagram there is a code, for example 1, e2-e4 by King Kashem's first move. Knowledge of this code (or 'notation') is not required for you to be able to follow the game: you can simply copy the moves from the diagrams onto your own board. However, it is very useful to be able to understand chess notation, so you may like to take a look at the explanation on page 40.

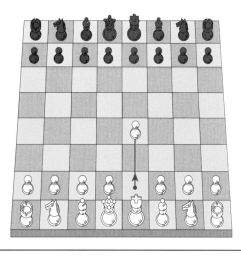

1. e2-e4
King Kashem's opening move is to send one of his pawns out to occupy a square in the centre of the board.

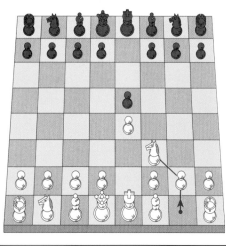

2. Ng1-f3
'Now I will attack that advanced black pawn with one of my knights,' decided Kashem.

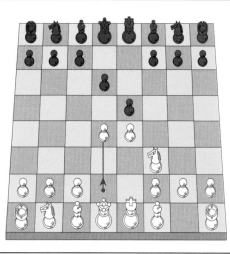

3. d2-d4
'Moving you forward clears a path for our bishop, and attacks a black pawn at the same time.'

'This will be your last war, Baduraul. If I win, you will return to your own country and leave my people in peace! That is what we have agreed.' Kashem too was feeling strong and confident of success.

Kashem was to play with the white pieces, and Baduraul with the black. This had been decided by the toss of a coin. It was Kashem's first move, since he was playing white. Then it would be Baduraul's turn.

black

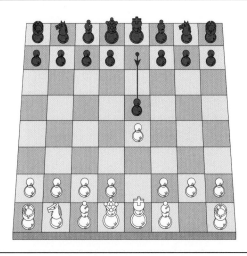

1. ..... e7-e5
King Baduraul also orders one of his pawns to the centre of the board, to stop the white pawn advancing any further.

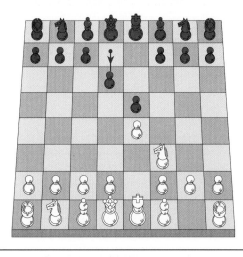

2. ..... d7-d6
'Go and defend your brother!' said Baduraul, advancing a second pawn.

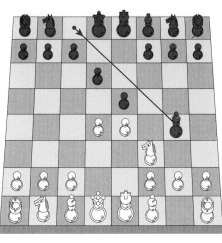

3. ..... Bc8-g4
Baduraul sends one of his fast-moving bishops to the battle front in order to attack the white knight.

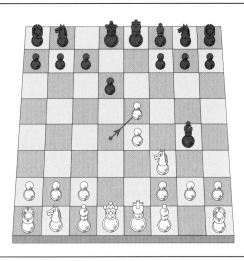

4. d4xe5
'We cannot move the knight, because then the bishop would take our queen. But we can still capture that pawn in the centre.'

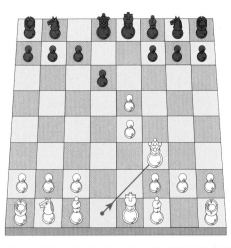

5. Qd1xf3
The queen is threatened, but King Kashem orders her to capture the bishop, so that the threat is removed.

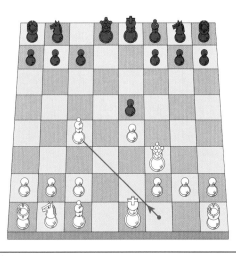

6. Bf1-c4
'Our queen is attacking the pawn which protects the black king; let us join her in the attack with our bishop.'

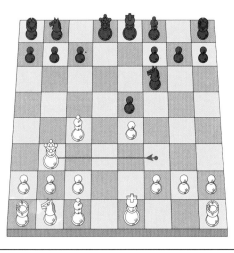

7. Qf3-b3
'So, let us double up the threat on that black pawn again.'

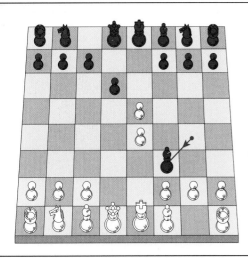

4. ..... Bg4xf3
'Bishop, take that white knight prisoner!'

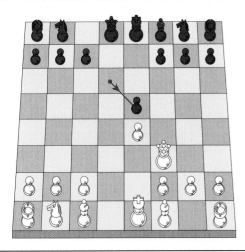

5. ..... d6xe5
'Away with the intruder that captured our pawn!'

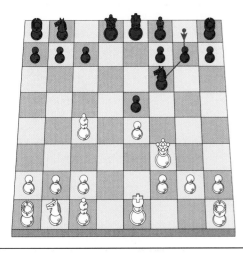

6. ..... Ng8-f6
'This is looking dangerous,' said Baduraul. 'Knight, go and protect our threatened pawn by standing in front of him.'

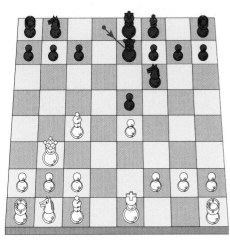

7. ..... Qd8-e7
'Another double attack! This Kashem likes to play rough. Time to help out with my queen.'

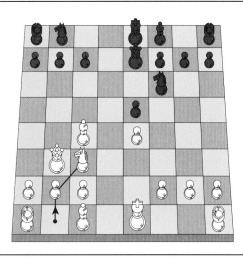

8. Nb1-c3
'Knight, time for you to join in the fight. We will have to use all our forces if we want to win.'

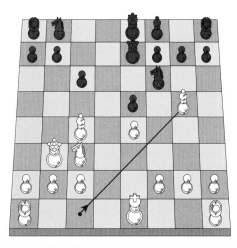

9. Bc1-g5
'Hmm, I don't think Baduraul is playing so well. He is taking too long to get his main soldiers into the action.'

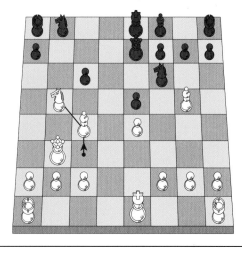

10. Nc3xb5
'Baduraul still hasn't taken his king out of danger. Let's sacrifice a knight to make room for the attack!'

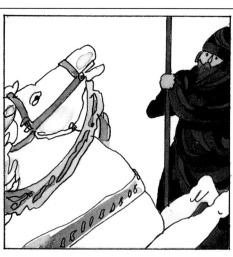

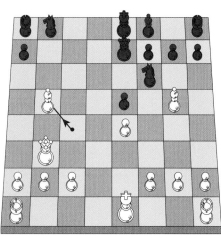

11. Bc4xb5+
'Bishop takes pawn. Check!'

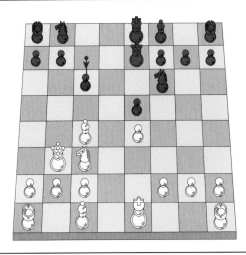

8. ..... c7-c6
'One step forward, pawn. This way our queen can defend its fellow soldier on b7.'

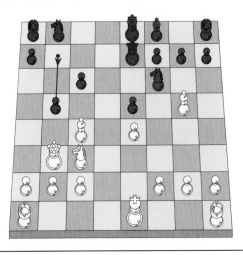

9. ..... b7-b5
'That bishop of Kashem's is looking too strong. Time to chase him off.'

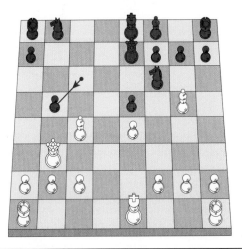

10. ..... c6xb5
'What a stupid move. That knight is worth much more than my pawn. Pawn takes knight, thanks very much!'

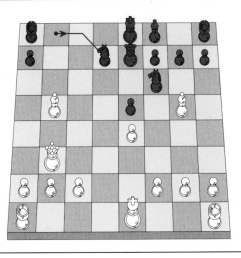

11. ..... Nb8-d7
'Have no fear, my king. I shall protect you!' cries the knight as he places himself in front of the black king.

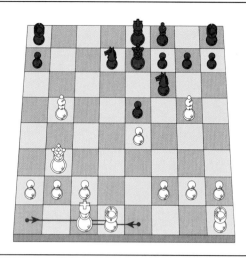

12. O-O-O
'By castling on the queen's side, my king is safer, and now my rook can join in the attack as well.'

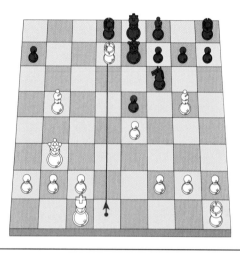

13. Rd1xd7
'This move clears the way for my second rook to join the fight.'

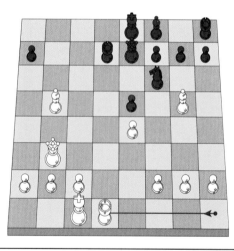

14. Rh1-d1
'Now for the second rook. Attack, my friend!'

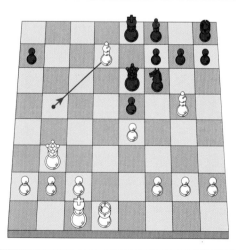

15. Bb5xd7+
'Check! The black bishop has entered the game far too late. I shall teach him a lesson!'

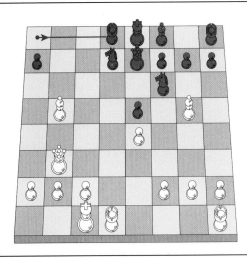

12. ..... Ra8-d8
'Kashem is forcing me to go on the defensive,' thought Baduraul. 'Rook, come and help immediately!'

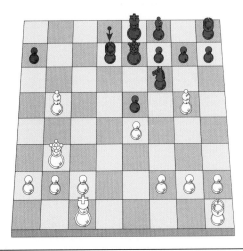

13. ..... Rd8xd7
'This is the only move I can make,' mumbled Baduraul. 'I don't want to capture with my queen, she is far too precious.'

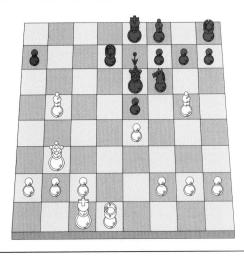

14. ..... Qe7-e6
'I will move my queen out of the way for a moment so the bishop can join the battle.'

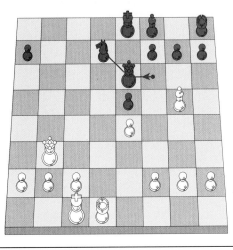

15. ..... Nf6xd7
'Do not worry, my king. I, your knight, am always ready for action.'

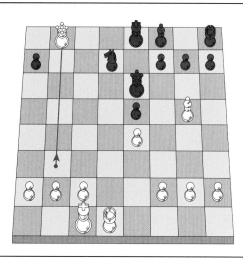

16. Qb3-b8+
'Check! Even if it costs me my queen, I must play to win!' cried Kashem. 'And I think victory is within my grasp.'

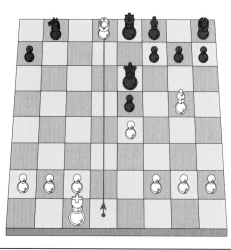

17. Rd1-d8++
'Yes, Baduraul, it was indeed a trap. Your king cannot escape. Checkmate!'

The valley of the Chenab lay peacefully under the midday sun.
King Baduraul had held counsel, and withdrawn his army.
Little Kalem walked through the fertile fields beside King Kashem.
'One day all this will be yours,' said King Kashem.
'You saved the country, and you have earned the right
to be king when I am no longer here.'
'Fine by me, Sire,' replied Kalem. 'And in the meantime, how about a
game of chess, just for the fun of it?'

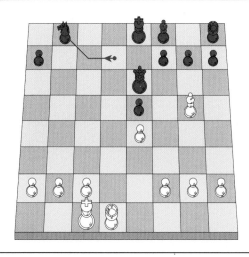

16. ..... Nd7xb8
'How foolish of
Kashem to give away
his queen like that.
I hope it is not a
trap!'

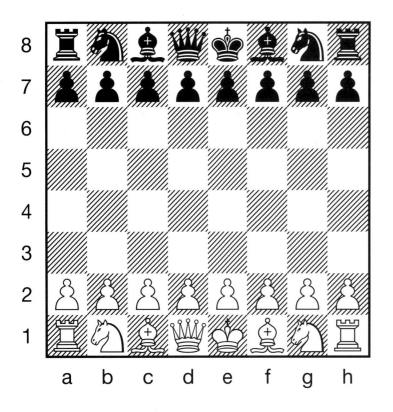

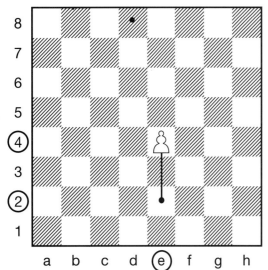

You are sure to have seen the picture of the chessboard opposite at some time in the newspaper.

Chessplayers throughout the whole world use this kind of picture, called a *diagram*. It has been agreed to draw the pieces in the same way in all diagrams, so that everyone can recognise them.

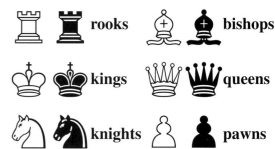

When you move a piece, there is a special way of describing exactly where the piece is moved to which everybody can easily understand. Every square has its own code, which you can find by looking at the numbers on the side (1 to 8) and the letters on the bottom (a to h) of the chessboard. At the start of the game for example, white has a rook in the square in the bottom left corner, which has the code a1, and in the top right corner there is a black rook on h8. The *diagram* shows how a pawn moves from square e2 to square e4; you write this down as: 'e2-e4'. To show which piece is being moved, you use the first letter of the name of the piece, except in the case of the pawn and the knight. For pawns no letter at all is used. And for the knight an 'N' is used, so you will not confuse it with the king. K is for king, Q for queen, R for rook, B for bishop, and N for knight. Castling on the king's side is written as O-O, and on the queen's side as O-O-O. When a piece captures another piece on its move, then we put an 'x' between the two codes, e.g. 'Bg4xf3'. Now you can write down all your games, and play them through again later. You will be a bit slow noting down your moves at first, but you soon get used to finding the right codes for the squares.

Every move in the game between Kashem and Baduraul has been written down, just as it should be. Good luck!

Try these two games:

1. e2-e4	e7-e5	1. f2-f4	e7-e5
2. Ng1-f3	d7-d6	2. f4xe5	d7-d6
3. Bf1-c4	Bc8-g4	3. e5xd6	Bf8xd6
4. c2-c3	Nb8-c6	4. Nb1-c3?	Qd8-h4+
5. Qd1-b3	Bg4xf3?	5. g2-g3	Qh4xg3+
6. Bc4xf7+	Ke8-e7	6. h2xg3	Bd6xg3++
7. Qb3-e6++			

New symbols:

+	check	!	strong move
++	checkmate	?	weak move